**THE SWEDISH
ART OF WELL-BEING
AND MINDFUL LIFE**

**NOT TOO MUCH,
NOT TOO LITTLE, JUST**

LAGOM

TOBIAS JAN

PEDERSEN

Copyright © 2022 Tobias Jan Pedersen

All Rights Reserved

TABLE OF CONTENTS

Introduction 5
Chapter 1: What is Lagom? 7
    Lagom Origin 7
    Lagom Myth Busting 8
    Why Choose Lagom Living 9
    The Key Benefits of Lagom 10
Chapter 2: Embracing Lagom Home Life 11
    Clean + Clutter-Free 12
    Eating Lagom 13
        Kanelbullar (Cinnamon Buns) 14
        Seeded Rye Bread 16
        Västerbotten Cheese Quiche 18
    Strawberry Meringue Cake 20
    Drinking Lagom 22
    Glögg (Mulled wine) 22
        Elderflower Cooler 26

Lemonade 28
Design and Interiors... 29
Chapter 3: Work-Life 33
Work-Life Balance 33
The Key to Success.. 35
Spiritual Life.. 35
Physical Life 38
    Physical Happiness 38
    Health and Wellbeing 38
    Exercise 43
    Personal Life.. 44
    Romantic Relationships.. 45
    Parenting... 47
    Friendships 55
    Celebrations.. 57
Chapter 4: Practice and Live Lagom... 64
The Environment and Sustainability 65
    Respecting Nature... 66
    Help Save The Bees! 71
    Protect The Trees! 73
    Establishing Yourself in A Community 75
    Saving Energy at Home The Lagom Way!................................ 78
    Your Home-energy Use.. 80
    Adopt New Energy-Saving Habits 81
    Reducing Your Foodprint The Lagom Way!............................ 84
    Eco-Friendly Shopping... 89
Conclusion 92

INTRODUCTION

You can use the word Lagom in pretty much any context, and without a doubt, you have probably already been practicing aspects of Lagom without even realizing it. Whether you work a lagom amount or your best shirt is a lagom fit, lagom is a deeply ingrained concept that is a part of the Swedish psyche. Today Lagom is almost directly linked to Swedish culture and their social ideology of equality and fairness.

Whether applied to leisure, work, family and relationships, holidays and celebrations, interior design, or simply living in a way that benefits the health and well-being of the planet, Swedes will often Lagom är bäst; meaning 'the right amount' and 'moderation is key. That being said, the Swedish always have time for excessiveness. However, they will not take it to the extreme; they will simply continue in moderation until the next party or celebration comes along.

Therefore, when it comes to finding a balance that suits you, it might be time to ask yourself some questions like; what is lagom? Why should you care? And if so, how can you adapt it into your everyday life? With these questions in mind, this book provides you with ideas to assist you in thinking more consciously about introducing Lagom in other ways too.

From 'what is Lagom' to 'practicing and Living Lagom,' and a few myths to bust here and there; this book, we prepare to "Logomify" our lives by deliberately seeking a more comfortable, manageable, and balanced way of doing things. By doing so, you're not just taking the pressure off yourself but off of others too. All the while gaining back one of life's most valuable resources; Time!.

CHAPTER 1: WHAT IS LAGOM?

In an era with so much to distract us in our overstimulated lives, wouldn't it be nice if we could turn to Lagom as an appreciative and conscious approach to living? Lagom is all about making a good life less complicated. As such, you may be under the impression that Lagom sounds exhausting; however, this is as far from the truth as you can likely get.

Lagom is as simple as placing a candle on a windowsill to welcome someone home. Lagom is both an inner and outer condition of simplicity, an honest, uncomplicated practice, and a clarity of presence and intention, even if it is simply taking a moment to enjoy a Fika.

Lagom Origin

Lagom has no direct translation; however, the word can loosely be translated to "not too little, not too much, but just enough."

It is widely believed that the word was derived from Viking times, rooted in the term "Laget om" (meaning around the team), and derives from the custom of passing a horn of mead around and ensuring that there was just enough for everyone to get a sip.

Although this may be true, the true derivation of the word suggests a relation to an old etymology of the word Lag, a common sense type of "Law."

Lagom Law

Not sure as to what exactly the law of lagom is? Well, the straightforward answer is the word describes something that's "Just right" or "Just enough,"-Like the perfect pressure of a massage or just the right amount of milk in your coffee or tea.

Looking past the material world, it becomes far more sophisticated, implying that the balancing act has reached perfection and relies on different societal norms.

That being said, Lagom is accepting an invitation to spend the day or weekend at a friend's house but bringing your own bed sheets, so you don't burden them with your laundry. It's having the right to stay at home with a sick child pay-intact without abusing that right.

Putting The Law Of Lagom Into Practice

Lagom focuses extensively on decluttering, simplifying life, erasing prejudice, and paving the way for honesty. As they often say, "Honesty is the best policy."

The balance of Lagom goes way beyond interior design and emotional well-being, although they too play a crucial role in understanding Lagom as a whole. Lagom is all about shared responsibility and belonging-not just fitting in, but being part of a more significant entity.

This also includes forming good relationships with your neighbors, looking after communal spaces, and paying your taxes.

Lagom Myth Busting

MYTH: Lagom celebrates mediocrity

Lagom is unimpressed by individual achievement and surplus wealth since lagom is all about finding what works for the collective and doing that well. However, all results are far from mediocre. In fact, they've contributed to one of the best social welfare systems in the world.

MYTH: Lagom enforces conformity through a thought-police state

Swedes tend to be highly opinionated and will happily engage in a calm, rational debate for hours on end, to an extent which the outsider might find infuriating. However, the end goal is not the arguments in itself but the arrival of a decision everyone can get behind. That approach may seem tabloid; however, this is hugely effective as far as the Lagom society is concerned.

MYTH: Lagom causes stinginess

For this myth, let's look at the old Swedish comic strip Spara och slösa, roughly translating to "saving and wasting." This Swedish comic strip aimed to teach children the importance of saving money. The cartoon was commissioned in the late 1920s by one of Sweden's leading banks and should be interpreted correctly.

This means that the cartoon does not celebrate stinginess. While mindless spending sprees and excessive extravagance are frowned upon, find a new gadget that's been vigorously checked and awarded "best in test," and you'll soon see everyone jumping on the bandwagon.

Why Choose Lagom Living

According to happiness research, money can make us happy however this is only to a certain degree. If we are poor, money can add to our sense of happiness; however, if you are already well off, it is most likely that gaining more of it won't make you happier in the long run.

A Lagom amount of money is just enough; beyond that, your happiness levels depend on other factors. You could perhaps say that Lagom is a timely trend. Most people are under enormous amounts of stress, spending too much time staring at their screens and regretting spending time with friends and family.

When it comes to a Lagom living style, living lagom can significantly improve your sense of well-being, not to mention practicing Lagom can strengthen the relationships and bonds that you have with friends and family.

The Key Benefits of Lagom

Mental Space

When you learn to take a step back and stop your mind from spiraling, you can live life in a more focused and authentic way-embracing and coping with good and bad experiences and being fully present both at home and at work.

Physical Space

Try to moderate conscious consumption; this helps to make decluttering easier. This, in turn, turns your home into a more peaceful space where one can sit back and relax. With minimal Scandinavian design to boot, you may never want to leave the comforts of your home again.

A Sense of Well-Being

From improved relationships with your friends and neighbors to trust in society's collective and shared responsibilities, a Lagom attitude can help you feel a part of something bigger and help provide you with a sense of purpose and belonging.

Improved Finances

As you start to become increasingly more conscious, not only of your personal needs but also those of the planet, you'll be more likely to consume less while also learning to look after and be thrifty with your resources.

CHAPTER 2: EMBRACING LAGOM HOME LIFE

It has been said that happiness begins at home; either way, research shows that our environment affects our stress levels. If there is perhaps one area in which the Swedes have triumphed in it would be the home, the typical Scandinavian home is the essence of Lagom.

In other words, the Swedes have the balance just right but how so? Our Nordic friends exercise a considerable amount of restraint in their everyday homes lives. Walls are often colored in shades of white or light gray; nothing is ever too loud or bold, just calm.

Furniture and accessories are carefully thought out, too, with nothing too superfluous or with an over-the-top design. Ultimately your home becomes a little oasis, essentially a haven that you can escape to, to get away from the daily bustle of everyday life.

Clean + Clutter-Free

When we talk about the Swedes, it is safe to say that they have a natural ability to maintain an uncluttered home. To put it simply, they don't possess much stuff, and most Swedes tend not to hoard to keep their home decluttered. If we want to live a Lagom way of life, we first need to rid ourselves of all the things that may be cluttering up our home.

Signs You Need to Declutter

You have an entire cupboard or room with items that you never use.

You wish for extra space for storing your unused items.

It takes you longer than five minutes to find what you are looking for.

You feel stressed at the thought of friends, family, or perhaps even a loved one coming over to spend the day.

You own items or accessories that you neither use nor find joy in.

You may be lucky enough to have a neat haven, and if so, lucky you! However, if you have checked more than one of the boxes above, there is work that can be done to leave your home less cluttered.

Nine Simple Ways to Declutter Your Home

Start by creating a declutter to-do list, crossing off each task as you go on.

Start with one room at a time and move on to the next.

Dedicate ten minutes each day to one task. ("Slow and steady wins the race")

Use the "One in, One out' method where, for everything you buy, one thing goes.

Reduce the area where clutter can perhaps accumulate. (Dedicate a container for toiletries or a file for paperwork etc.)

Create a memory box.

Keep a basket.

Fill a bag a day with items you may no longer need or perhaps use.

Stick to the 'One-touch rule' for paperwork and sort it out as soon as it arrives.

Eating Lagom

Fika Lagom-style

In a culture otherwise keen on healthy eating and balanced meals, Fika adds a silver lining. On an ordinary Sunday, a cookie might suffice, however with Fika, this tradition calls for pulling out all the stops. As part of a playdate, Fika may include fruit and open sandwiches before the cinnamon buns come out.

However, on a typical weekend, Fika focuses all on the goodies. For instance, think about a table full of cookies and cakes, complete with pretty candles and coffee cups.

Fika to the Swedes is what pubs are to the Brits, a break from doing.

At a time when we receive constant social media notifications and work emails, Fika can be a way in which you take a break, relax and connect with yourself, friends, family, and perhaps even a loved one. Leave out the endless top-ups, and Fika will seem very Lagom indeed, compared to a night out.

NOTE: *The Swedes do indulge, but not too much. This, in turn, means you are more than welcome to help yourself to one type of each cookie; however, it's important to remember that you can't grab two slices of cake and never ever the last one of anything. It takes a non Swede or child to empty all the plates during a typical Fika session; otherwise, the last cookie will always stay put.*

Kanelbullar (Cinnamon Buns)

No one baked treat or pastry says Fika time as much as cinnamon-flavored buns, paired here with a touch of Cardamom. Think about that warm, spicy scent spreading throughout your home whilst the buns are baking in the oven. You'll soon begin to understand why the Swedes have an almost sacred relationship with Cinnamon.

Makes Ten Buns:

Ingredients:

- Sunflower oil for oiling
- One egg lightly beaten
- One and a ¾ oz Superfine sugar (49.6g)
- ½ a teaspoon fine salt (2.8g)
- ⅓ of a Packet of fast-action dried yeast (Your choice)
- One and ⅓ oz Butter (49.6g)
- 15 oz plain flour + extra for dusting (425.2g)
- One teaspoon ground Cardamom (5g)
- 10 oz Milk (295ml)

For The Filling:

- Two and a ¾ oz Butter softened (78g)
- One and a ¾ oz Light brown sugar (49.6g)
- Two teaspoons ground cinnamon (10g)
- ½ a teaspoon fine salt (2.5g)

For The Glaze:

- Raw sugar, for sprinkling
- One egg, lightly beaten

Preparation:

Lightly oil a large baking sheet or nine pie tins that measure about three and a ¼ inches (8.2cm) in diameter. Add the milk into a small saucepan, add the Cardamom and bring to just below boiling point. Switch off the heat, stir in the butter until melted, and leave the mixture to sit aside until warm.

Grab all your dry ingredients and mix them together into a large bowl. Make a well in the middle of the flour using your fingertips, add the egg, then stir in the warm milk mixture. Gradually mix all the ingredients until they are well combined, and a soft, sticky dough forms that should come away from the side of the bowl.

Place the dough on a lightly oiled work surface (DONT FLOUR IT) and knead by hand for five minutes. The dough will be very soft and sticky at first but will become less sticky with kneading. You can alternatively use a stand mixer fitted with a dough hook. Lightly oil a bowl and add the dough to it.

Cover the dough tightly with cling film or a clean tea towel and set aside to rise in a warm area for roughly 30-60 minutes. The time may vary depending on the temperature of the given day, so be sure to let the dough double in size. Whilst the dough is rising, you can make the filling.

Beat all the ingredients for the fling into a separate bowl until soft and easily spreadable, set aside for later. Roll the dough out onto a rectangular surface that is lightly floured, measuring about 14x10 inches

(355.6cm) and ⅛ inches (0.32cm) thick. Spread the Cinnamon filling over the dough and roll the dough up tightly, like a Swiss roll ending with a seam underneath.

Cut into ten slices around one inch (2.54cm) thick. Place the dough onto the baking sheet, leaving a small space in between them and the cover, and leave them to prove in a warm place for about 30 minutes. (Time may vary) The dough should spring back when prodded gently.

For the glaze, brush the buns with the beaten egg and add sugar to your liking. Meanwhile, start preheating the oven to 300°F or 149°C. Bake the buns for 25-30 minutes or until golden brown. Place the buns evenly onto a wire rack and set them aside to cool down. (Delicious when served warm too!)

Seeded Rye Bread

From Smörgåsboard spreads to solid breakfasts and open sandwiches, a slice of good, healthy rye bread is a must-have for any aspiring Lagom enthusiast.

Makes: One (9x5) inch or (114.3cm) loaf

Ingredients:

- Two and a ¾ oz (78g) Linseeds/Flaxseeds
- Two and a ¾ oz (78g) Sunflower seeds
- Two and a ¾ oz (78g) Cracked rye or Rye flakes
- Two Teaspoons (10ml) Dark syrup or Black treacle
- Two Teaspoons (10g) Fast-action dried yeast or your preferred choice
- 18 oz (510g) Boiling water
- Two Teaspoons (10g) of fine salt
- 9 oz (255g) White rye flour + extra for dusting
- 9 oz (255g) dark rye flour
- Sunflower oil for oiling

Preparation:

Lightly oil a 9x5 inch (114.3cm) loaf tin and set it aside. Mix the dry ingredients together, such as the flour and salt, into a large bowl. Pour the boiling water you have measured into the bowl with the dry ingredients and begin mixing it until it's a thick, slightly crumbly paste. Set aside the mixture to cool for a little while.

Add the dried yeast and dark syrup or black treacle along with the cracked rye or rye flakes. Add most of the seeds, reserving a few to sprinkle onto the top. Stir in just enough water to bring the mixture together. It should be soft and not too sticky. Lay the dough out onto a work surface that has been lightly floured.

Knead the dough for about five minutes, or until all the ingredients have been thoroughly incorporated into the dough. You can also opt to utilize a stand mixer fitted with a dough hook to make things easier. Shape the dough into a sausage shape, roughly the same length as the tin that you'll be using.

Place the dough inside the tin and brush with a bit of water sprinkling over the leftover seeds. Cover the dough using a clean damp cloth and leave it in a warm, draft-free space for several hours, preferably overnight, to play it safe. The dough will rise without doubling in size; it should only rise by about a quarter.

Once you are ready to bake, begin by first preheating the oven to 400°F or 204°C. When the oven has finished preheating, place a roasting tray half-filled with boiling water into the bottom of the oven. Bake the bread in the oven for roughly 35-40 minutes, or until the top has been well browned. The base should sound hollow when tapped.

Place the bread onto a wire rack and let the bread cool entirely before slicing. (Can be served hot)

Västerbotten Cheese Quiche

Quiches suit the Lagom approach to eating not only because they work well as part of a buffet but simply by being versatile. They're also perfect for bringing along to a picnic or Potluck. This matured-cheese version is well suited for special occasions and celebrations.

Serves: Six (or more if part of a buffet)

Ingredients:

- Two Tablespoons (30ml) cold water
- Four and a ½ oz (127.5g) Diced, cold salted butter
- Six oz (170g) Plain flour

For the Filling:

- Freshly grounded black pepper
- Pinch of salt
- Five and a ½ oz (156g) Västerbottensost* cheese, grated
- Five oz (148ml) Double cream
- Three and a ½ oz (103.5ml) Milk
- Three eggs

Preparation:

Preheat the oven to 218°C or 425°F

To make the pastry, add the flour and butter into the bowl rubbing together with your fingertips until you have a crumbly texture. Add the water you have measured and combine the ingredients to form a smooth dough. Press the dough into a nine and a ½ inch (24cm) round pie or quiche tin.

If you have a loose-bottomed one, you can use that. Prick the base of the pastry gently with a fork and bake for 10-12 minutes or until golden. For the filling, whisk the eggs, milk, and cream in a bowl until all the ingredients are well combined, then stir in the grated cheese.

Season to your liking with salt and pepper, and then pour the filling into the pastry case. Bake for 20 minutes or until the filling has been set and leave aside to cool.

NOTE: *Västerbottensost is widely available in several stores outside of Sweden. If you can't find the real deal try substituting your mature cheese of choice with half mature Cheddar and half Parmesan, this works well too.*

Strawberry Meringue Cake

My mother's Strawberry meringue cake always takes me back to my childhood memories, eating cake with my friends and drinking lemonade in the hot summer sun. However, this Swedish classic works just as well for a midsummer celebration or perhaps a Summer party or even "Fika."

Serves: 10-12

Ingredients: (For the sponge cake)

- Two Teaspoons (10g) of baking powder
- Five and a ½ oz (150g) Plain flour
- One and ¾ oz (49,6g) Butter, melted and cooled
- Five5 Tablespoons (75ml) of milk
- One Tablespoon (15g) vanilla sugar
- Five and a ½ oz (150g) Superfine sugar
- Three Egg yolks

- Sunflower oil for oiling

For The Meringue:

Ingredients:

- Two and a ¼ oz (64g) Blanched almonds, chopped
- Five and a ½ oz (150g) Superfine sugar
- Four Egg whites

For The Filling and Topping:

- 14 oz (400g) Strawberries, hulled and sliced
- 14 oz (415ml) Double cream or whipped cream

Preparation:

Preheat the oven to approximately 350°F or 177°C and line two, eight-inch (20cm) cake tins with baking paper. Next, lightly brush with oil.

For the sponge cake, whisk the egg yolks, superfine sugar, and vanilla extract together in a large mixing bowl until the eggs are fluffy and pale in color. Then mix in the melted butter and milk. Sift both the baking powder and flour into a bowl, then gently fold into the whisked mixture. Spread the batter evenly out onto the two cake tins.

For the meringue, in a large separate, super clean, grease-free bowl, whisk the egg whites until stiff peaks form, then add in the superfine sugar and mix until thick and glossy. This will result in a nice chewy meringue. Next, spread the meringue mixture across the cake batter, then sprinkle with the chopped almonds—Bake for 20 minutes or until golden brown.

Let the cake cool off for 10 -15 minutes or longer, depending on the temperature of that given day. Peel off the wax lining paper and let it sit while you start your next task.

Gently whip the cream with a whisk or electric mixer (on medium) until soft peaks form. Now, place one cake half on a plate and top with half the cream and strawberries. Top the other half with the remaining strawberries and cream. You can add more almonds at this point, or you can eat it as is. Both are delectable.

Vanilla sugar is more commonly used in baked Northern European cuisine; however, you can always substitute this with vanilla extract if your local convenience store does not have it.

Drinking Lagom

When we think of Lagom, food is essentially the first thing that comes to mind; however, what about drinks? Here we will look at three simple Swedish drinks, Glögg, otherwise known as Mulled wine, Elderflower cordial, and an Elderflower cooler.

Glögg (Mulled wine)

Advent is a very special time in Sweden, during the four Sundays before Christmas. The Swedes start lighting candles, bake in preparation for the festive season and adorn their windows with star lights and Advent candelabra. At the same time, Christmas itself can often feel like one big overwhelming feast, with most people going all out with lavish feasts and casseroles.

It will come as no surprise to find out that most Swedes prefer Advent over Christmas day as this is a more restrained time to indulge in some Lagom cuisine. This can't happen without some Glögg to add to the Christmas spirit.

Serves: About 15 (Small cups)

Ingredients:

- ½ a teaspoon (2.5g) Cardamom pods
- Ten Cloves
- Two Cinnamon sticks
- One Piece of a bitter orange peel
- Two small pieces of ginger or One inch (2.54cm) of peeled fresh ginger
- Nine oz (266ml) Unsweetened apple juice
- Six oz (177ml) Bottle of Red wine

To Serve:

- Orange slices
- Star anise
- Cinnamon sticks
- Raisins and whole blanched almonds (Optional)

Preparation:

Place all of the ingredients into a saucepan, except those to serve, and heat the mixture over low heat. You should begin to see steam rising from the top of the mixture; keep stirring frequently and keep a watchful eye on the mixture, making sure that it doesn't boil.

Turn the heat off, let the mixture sit overnight for a solid 16 hours. Once you are ready to serve, gently reheat and serve in little cups garnished with orange slices. Add your cinnamon sticks, star anise, and sprinkle with a few raisins and blacked almonds, if liked. (Cheers or Skål!)

NOTE: This drink is an alcoholic beverage and is not intended to be drunk by anyone under the ages of 18 and 21; age may vary depending on the county you are from

KEYNOTE: *Skål is the traditional Danish, Swedish, and Norwegian term for a bowl. The word Skål is now also commonly used when toasting, "Cheers!"*

Elderflower Cordial

Elderflower is exceptionally versatile and refreshing, not to mention it's widely available in parks and fields if you fancy yourself a foraging session. (Unless, of course, you feel like cultivating some yourself and adding a beautiful addition to your garden or allotment.) With some Elderflower in the pantry, you'll be ready to please children at birthday parties and adults craving cocktails alike.

Makes about: Three and a ½ Pints (Two liters)

Ingredients:

Two lbs (900g) / Four oz (1.2L) Granulated sugar

One and ¾ pints (1L) Water

One oz (28g) Citric acid (Available online)

Three Lemons, sliced

20 Elderflower heads, shaken to remove any insects or bugs

Preparation:

Put the citric acid, lemon slices, and elderflower heads in a large, heatproof bowl. Add the water and sugar that you have measured into a large saucepan, slowly bring to a boil over low heat. Ensuring that the sugar has been fully dissolved into the solution, stirring occasionally.

Pour the sugar syrup over the ingredients that are in a bowl and stir well, let this cool down. Once the mixture is cool enough, add cling film and refrigerate overnight. This will infuse the mixture with the ingredient that you have added. Strain the mixture utilizing a fine metal sieve to make sure it's a fine sieve, as sieves with bigger holes can lead to some impurities spoiling your drink.

Once the mixture has been fully strained and you're happy with the clarity, bottle the mixture into sterilized airtight bottles. You can store this Elderflower cordial mixture for up to six months as long as it's in a cool, dry space.

NOTE: You can also make this drink into an alcoholic beverage. You can find the recipe below. Remember to always drink with caution to ensure simplicity and balance in every aspect of your life.

Elderflower Cooler

Whether you're throwing a BBQ or having a picnic in the garden, your homemade cordial (See above recipe) will come in handy for making a drink with a distinctive taste and refreshing kick. Just add your white spirit of choice and enjoy!

Serves: Six Depending on cup size

Ingredients:

- Cold water or soda water
- Elderflower cordial
- Ice cubes
- A few sprigs of mint
- Five Limes
- One Lemon

Preparation:

Squeeze a single lemon into a large jug or pitcher, and repeat the same process with the limes. Throw the squeezed-out fruits into the pitcher/jug along with the mint sprigs and ice cubes.

Fill the jug/pitcher with 1 part elderflower cordial to Ten parts of water, or soda water if you prefer a fizzier drink. Stir the mixture well and add in your spirit of choice. Let it sit and refrigerate for 16 hours or until the mixture has thoroughly chilled.

NOTE: This drink is an alcoholic beverage and is not intended to be drunk by anyone under the ages of 18 or 21; age may vary depending on the county you are from.

Lemonade

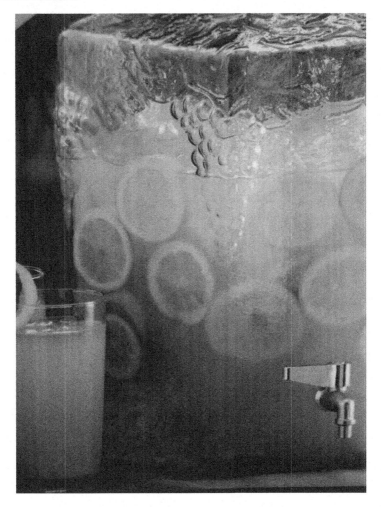

Serves: Six (Depending on cup size)

Ingredients:

- Two-Three Cups (470ml/ 710ml) cold water to dilute
- One cup (237ml) water for simple syrup
- One cup (210g) sugar
- Four-six Lemons (depending on size)
- Lemon slices and ice (optional)

Preparation:

Place both the water and sugar into a small saucepan and bring to a simmer. Stir gently and wait for the sugar to dissolve completely before turning off the heat. Begin juicing the lemons while the simple syrup is heating (can be done after) depending on the size of the lemons; four-six will be required to fill up one cup of lemon juice.

Next, pour the lemon juice and simple syrup into a glass serving pitcher. Add two-three cups of cold water and taste. If the blend is too sweet, add some more water. Chill in the refrigerator for 30-40 minutes or until the lemonade has been fully cooled to your liking. It can be served with thinly cut lemon slices and ice. (Optional)

Design and Interiors

When it comes to your home and the interiors, along with the design, it's important to remember that the Swedes tend to use lots of whites, grays, and rustic colors. Not only do these colors give off a warm feeling, but more often than most, they leave the house with a warmer/cozier atmosphere.

A feature wall embodies the Lagom approach to interiors, and you can even go for one wall in a different color or wallpaper. Simply put, doing the whole room might seem like a big task, but worry not as one wall is "Lagom."

Storage

It's easy to think along the lines that storage is evil; however, this is not the case. Think about entire wall cupboards or shelves put together in a stylistic modular combination or perhaps drawer units under the bed. The choice is yours to make, and making the best use of height is always a good option. So do some planning before any significant changes are made to the interiors of your apartment/home.

Mood-enhancing Interiors

Start by picking a neutral base with furniture and colors. These can be colors that you like and or admire for their bright appeal or contrast. You can then move items/furniture around your house/apartment to suit your current mood or the given season.

Keeping your home/apartment decluttered is a critical step in minimizing stress from your everyday workload. A handy tip from a Swede such as myself; "Start by creating a relaxing corner for yourself where you can recharge."

Lagom Cozy

You can opt to take up knitting or perhaps another hobby that you find interesting. The calming effect it has is addictive, and those long train rides to work will pass in no time. Trying out a hobby or two is a great way to relax. Not only will these hobbies tend to alleviate stress, but they can also add a personal touch to your home, which most store-bought items cannot.

You don't necessarily have to stop there; you can rummage through some of your parents' or grandparents' old stuff. Find an old picture frame or perhaps a coffee table. You can easily refashion these items into a charming, characterful interior detail with an interesting story to brag about to friends and family.

When it comes to Lagom, it would be in your best interests to keep things simple so pick a hobby that best suits you. No need to go out of your comfort zone. Stay within the margin that you feel most comfortable with.

Fashion and Style

When it comes to the swedes, most of them have a few things in common, the most crucial being that functionality and comfort always come first. Dressing and styling Lagom is all well and good; however, it is just as much about feeling comfortable as fitting in, in the most sophisticated ways.

Suffice to say that shoes made of plastic and garments that require hand washing are more than likely to be left on the shelves. When dressing

Lagom, it's crucial to think of loose and comfortable shapes, a darker color scheme (primarily black) with an odd attention-grabbing print or statement scarf.

Moreover, you can throw in some big jewelry, bright red lipstick, and peroxide-blonde hair accompanied by walking-friendly shoes and or brogues/sneakers. Behind this trendy look is a capsule wardrobe topped with black basics that work with everything, don't forget a few garments that stand out.

The Capsule Wardrobe

Loosely speaking, the Swedish wardrobe can be likened to a capsule wardrobe. A convenient, minimalist closet is created by clearing out unused or unwanted clothes and replacing them with a limited number of well-loved garments, which you can ultimately wear together.

A capsule wardrobe makes it easier to pick out an outfit; this also takes the stress out of getting dressed. This helps you spend less time picking an outfit to wear, not to mention spending less time and energy on shopping and laundry.

The Cultural Lady

Kulturtant (loosely translated to "the culture lady") style is typically made up of bright but nature-inspired colors, linen, and other natural materials. Don't forget the layers and layers of loose fabrics. While the Kulturtant may be a far cry from the sophisticated Söermalm style, it is Lagom in several ways.

Perhaps mostly celebrating comfort and green thinking without restricting freedom of expression. Who said orange couldn't go with pink? The sustainable capsule wardrobe works just as well with garments of all colors. The Swedes have become natural experts at dressing practically. Not only this but the style is based on comfort with varied details of understated cuts.

It has been said that the Swedes stand out in the Lagom way of less is more. You may find that at home, the trend-conscious part of the population is like a monochrome mass; however, if you go abroad, you can almost instantly spot a Swede in a crowd. This low-key style almost seems extravagant to some, but not most Swedes.

Lagom Fashion Statement

So, what is the cultural status of the "Swedes"? For a long time, its primary focus has been centered around not expressing status at all. The Swedes have rarely used garments to canvas for colors, messages, or patterns, which you can often see in most Italian fashion styles.

Clothes are generally viewed by most of the population as consumables, they are for everyone, and things that are for everyone must be Lagom- not too colorful, not too crazy. It can be a bit boring or perhaps quite liberating. Simply put, it's like spending a casual everyday Friday at home where everyone can relax more.

When it comes to the cultural status of the Swedes, if you would like to make a statement opt for eco-friendly clothes that are natural as well as colors that aren't too bright; however, feel free to express yourself through clothes that you find comfortable to wear, as everyone's sense of comfort differs.

CHAPTER 3: WORK-LIFE

When it comes to Lagom, it's important to remember to keep your work life in order and try to accomplish tasks that are given to you on time. It's essential to not rush any given task at work and balance out your time wisely, factoring in all other daily activities that you might have on a set day.

Work-Life Balance

When balancing your work and life, there are a couple of ways to achieve the balance, such as becoming an early bird, taking breaks, and a couple of things you can do during your lunchtime. Becoming an early bird has numerous advantages, from becoming more proactive as well as having more time to spend on other activities during the course of the day.

This, in turn, can lead to you becoming more creative as an individual, not to mention you'll have more time on your hands.

Four Reasons to Become an Early Bird:

- *Time to exercise:* The first few hours in the morning might be the only time you have to exercise, so why not take the opportunity to do so. This can help give you an early-morning energy boost and can help you to become more productive afterwards.

- *You'll be happier:* Yes, this is indeed true as a study by the University of Toronto shows that individuals who tend to wake up earlier are more than likely to be happier than night owls.

- *Fewer distractions:* With fewer distractions, you'll have more time to spend on yourself, whether that be by reading a newspaper or perhaps having an early yoga session. You can even get an early start with work and check a few emails or perhaps start a task early.

- ***Time for breakfast:*** Breakfast has been considered the most important meal of the day. Waking up early often gives you more time to relax while you eat. In the same vein, it helps you kick the day off with a healthy start.

Take a Break

Take a step inside a Swedish workplace, and you will notice how quiet it is. Everyone's beavering away, and there isn't any idle chat or persistent hum. You will be greeted by a cheerful wave and might even encounter the odd huddle of people talking in hushed voices.

However, more often than most, the topic is work-related, as, in Swedish offices, most of the social chit chat is reserved for breaks. You'll be surprised to know that the Swedish even have a name for the work break called "Fikapaus' ' Which loosely translates to a break with coffee and perhaps even a little treat.

There is even another term called "Fika," which loosely translates to afternoon coffee or tea break; however, these are generally scheduled for ten in the morning and three in the afternoon. Taking a break in itself is not wrong, so don't feel shy to do so.

Five Great Things to do at Lunchtime

In our day to day busy lives, time is precious, we have to make every second count, and we should be mindful of how we use our time. The lunch break is no different, and depending on the contract you have; you can have anywhere from 30-60 minutes of free time.

If you are not embarrassed to embrace the Swedish ethos of taking a decent break, there's usually time left after eating, so spend that time exactly as you please. Take this time to use the spare time you have wisely. You'll not only enhance your well-being; you'll boost your career, too!

1. ***Indulge in the arts:*** Visit a local museum, or perhaps take up photography using an app on your phone or even read a book; the choice is yours. This will take your mind off work and will help you relax if you have had a stressful day at work.

2. *Arrange a date:* Invite a friend that lives nearby or perhaps a work colleague, and talk to your heart's content about life and any other topic of interest that you both share.

3. *Get your blood pumping:* Go for jogs or power walks, or perhaps attend your daily lunchtime gym glass if your workplace has these facilities. If not, you can always opt to go to a local gym nearby. This will help re-energize you before your afternoon shift.

4. *Meditate:* Find a quiet spot that you can meditate in. It will help alleviate symptoms of stress and help declutter your brain, preparing your mind, body, and soul for the daily shift.

5. *Don your headphones and play your favorite toons:* Listening to music lights up your entire brain, and it has been said that this releases endorphins into the brain leading to a more positive outlook on life. This has been linked to feeling a greater sense of well-being and can, in turn, leave you feeling more productive and perhaps even more intelligent.

The Key to Success

The majority of individuals equate success with a prosperous career and a million in the bank. I would most likely have done the same before moving to Sweden. Perhaps the most liberating lesson out of all my experiences during my stay here would be the feeling of being satisfied with "enough."

If you have a mindset that is set on thinking that having more is equal to happiness, you'll always be left wanting. *By building a life centered around less materialistic items, you'll feel less stress and pressure.* This can help you find the freedom to focus on the more important things, such as friends, family, and loved ones.

Spiritual Life

When it comes to Lagom and spiritual life, keeping it simple isn't just about reading a book or going for a leisurely stroll. There can be numerous other activities where you can get in touch with yourself through meditation and or prayers.

These are just some ways in which you can get in touch with your spiritual life. If you'd want to delve a little deeper, you can always do some at-home research or consult with a professional, all in the comfort of your own home. What more could you need from Lagom?

Soothing Your Soul

Sleep is mother nature's way of helping us to declutter the mind and helps restore our bodies and souls. Without the proper amount of sleep, we function less effectively and damage our sense of well-being and health in the long run.

This is not the only way to create a balanced state of mind; you can even opt to go outside or plan a low-budget holiday which I've noticed can be a great antidote to a world that is constantly stressful.

Sleep

A lot can be said about a great night's sleep. You probably know those mornings when you wake up and feel well-rested and raring to go. Well, there are several critical factors involved in creating a calming pre-bedtime ritual.

So, what's the secret? Try to first prepare yourself both mentally and physically before going to bed, as stated by the Swedish psychologist *"Helena Kubicek Boye"* who is an expert on sleep psychology.

Preparing the Mind

What you plan to do before you go to bed is key to a successful slumber. A recent study shown in Norway found that screen time can affect your ability to fall asleep and reduces the quality of your slumber. So now that the latest series on *Netflix* is out of the question, what should you do before bed?

Pre-bedtime Activities:

- Cuddling up with family and pets
- Painting or (mindful coloring)

- Embroidery
- Knitting
- Listening to calm music
- Taking a warm bath
- Reading a book

Keep a Diary:

When the lights go out, more often than most, thoughts and worries creep in from the day. Keeping a journal is an effective way to reflect on the events that have occurred over the day.

Five Ways to Sleep Like a Swede:

1. ***Keep it calm:*** The Swedish bedroom, with its soft, muted color palette and minimalist furnishing, which gives off an airy feel, is the epitome of calm. Start off by adding white and light gray walls, pure linen bedding (great for keeping cozy in winter and cool in summer), and layers of natural textures for cooler evenings.

2. ***Keep it clean:*** Ensure your bedroom is clutter-free and try to avoid busy patterns in the decor.

3. ***Divide and conquer:*** Book yourself into a Swedish hotel, and you'll be surprised to notice single duvets instead of a double, and during my stay here, I've found this to be universal across all Swedish marital beds. Friends and family tell me that this allows you to choose a duvet cover with a thickness that is Lagom for you, which means you can stick those naked limbs out at a whim.

4. ***Go au naturel:*** Swedes commonly shun traditional nightwear and opt for a favorite pair of underwear. (Most of the time, nothing at all) Not only are the Swede's homes well insulated, but sleeping in less also helps you keep cool.

5. ***Create darkness:*** The sleep-inducing hormone melatonin is directly connected to the simulations around us. By darkening your room, you're telling your body it's ready and time to go to

sleep. Cover any LED lights and use blackout blinds to ensure a restless night's sleep.

Physical Life

We can't all be blessed with a flowing mane of golden hair and a gorgeous-looking body; however, we can always learn a thing or two from the Swedes about looking after our bodies. They take the no-nonsense approach, simply enjoying a balanced diet, neither denying themselves that cinnamon bun nor going overboard with the salad serving.

They also naturally incorporate exercise into their day, favoring the bike over a car or public transport, whether there's sun, rain, wind, or snow. So this means that even on the busiest of days, the Swedes have their hearts pumping!

Physical Happiness

There are copious ways in which we can achieve "Physical Happiness" such as;

- Going for jogs and walks
- Exercising at a local gym
- Riding your bike
- Join a local dojo or fitness center

Health and Wellbeing

When it comes to your health and personal well-being, it's essential to keep in mind what you eat and try your best to eat in moderation. This doesn't mean you have to shy away from snacks. An occasional snack here and there won't do you any harm.

Eating in Moderation

It would be safe to say that if you are not a fan of fish or potatoes, you might find it hard to cope in Sweden. No holiday smorgasbord is complete without them. National dishes or (husmanskost) include *sill och potatis* (a serving of Herring and potatoes with lingonberries), *köttbullar med potatismos* (Meatballs and mash), and *pyttipanna* (a mix of cubed potatoes, meat, and onions with a side of beetroot.)

Jokes aside, the Nordic diet has been fastly recognized for its health benefits. The average life expectancy in Sweden is on average 80 years for men and 84 years for women, which puts the country firmly in the top ten of the World Health Organization (WHO.)

Nordic meals are all about balance and seasonal produce. In fact, a study by the Nordic Center of Excellence (NCE) demonstrated that a healthy Nordic diet could improve cholesterol levels, lower the risk of corneal heart disease, and can help reduce inflammation. In other words, it is good for your waistline and heart.

Eat the Swedish Way

Crispbread

Known locally as knäckebröd, crispbread has been a staple in the Swedish diet since the late AD 500. In part, its popularity is thanks to its long expiration date and low price, But it has also been found to have health benefits. It is traditionally made with whole wheat-rye flour, salt, and water and is low in fat, high in fiber, and packed with vitamins, antioxidants, and minerals.

Lingonberry

Also known locally as cowberries, mountain berries, and partridge berries, lingonberries grow in the Noric forest and are enjoyed as jam, as a relish, or perhaps on top of pancakes. Not only are they Jam-packed with antioxidants (pun intended), Vitamins A and C, magnesium, and fibers, research at *Lund University* has found that they can also help regulate your metabolism.

Filmjölk

A traditional fermented milk, this healthy dairy product is commonly eaten with cereal at breakfast time or during lunch break. The lactic acid bacteria are considered to facilitate the digestive process, strengthen the immune system, and also reduce the risk of allergies.

Potatoes

A staple worldwide and in many different regions, the standard spud carries plenty of health benefits. This vegetable is rich in potassium (helps to lower blood pressure), fiber, and Vitamins B and C. Once cooked, this vegetable is high in resistant starch, which ultimately helps the body burn fat.

Herring

Smoked, fried, salted, or pickled, evidence suggests that the humble Herring has been a staple of the Nordic menu since Neolithic times. This small fish is relatively cheap and easy to store. It's also a great source of omega-3 fatty acids and Vitamin D, which has been known to prevent heart disease, boost the immune system, and can help the brain function at a higher level.

Rotten Fish

Although the Swedes have mastered the art of moderation, there is one thing that they even agree is far from Lagom. *Surströmming is famous everywhere for its overwhelmingly putrid smell and strong, acidic taste.* To put it simply, Herring is treated with just the right amount of salt to prevent it from going rancid.

Then the fish is left to sit for six months before it is tinned. The fermented Herring is served once a year (around the third Thursday of August) and consumed outdoors, preferably while holding your nose.

Exercise

You may be someone who likes to work up a sweat, perhaps after a 10km run or a session at the gym before breakfast. It can be hard to find the time of day to do so in our ever increasingly busy lives. No need to worry, though, as I've noticed that as a Lagom mindset, Swedes are adept at incorporating exercise into their daily lives without breaking a sweat.

Simply making a few changes here and there, like riding a bicycle instead of taking the train or walking instead of driving. You can start by making subtle changes, which can lead to an overall better sense of well-being. By making subtle changes, you'll find that it's Lagom.

Plogging

Plogging combines the Swedish verbs *plocka upp* (Pick up) and *jogga* (Jog) to give life to a new Swedish verb *plogga* from which the verb *plogging* derives. It is a relatively new exercise method that merges jogging with simultaneously picking up litter. As such, you are cleaning up the planet while you jog.

Talk about killing two birds simultaneously. Not only is this an effective method to keep healthy, but it's also a way in which you can help play your part in keeping your community clean and healthy. What began as a small organized event in Sweden in 2016 soon turned into a wide-scale event spanning different countries worldwide in 2018.

Why did such a trend take off? Well, as more and more people became concerned with the effect of plastic pollution on the environment, more and more people took up plogging. Plogging as a workout allows for a variety of body movements. This implies that you are either jogging, hiking, running or walking while also squatting, stretching, and bending simultaneously.

That being said plogging is quite an effective exercise routine, especially since it attracts more than 2 000 000 people in over 100 countries. Moreover, some plogging events can attract over 3 000 000 individuals. So, next time you decide to exercise, why not get together a group of friends or family members for a refreshing plogging session that benefits both you and the environment.

Personal Life

The respect that the Swedes have for their personal space and personal life in Sweden is mesmerizing and sometimes a little baffling. When it comes to making new friends and forming new friendships, the Swedes are slightly wary about coming off too strong.

This is why it's sometimes hard to form friendships; however, you'll develop a bond that lasts a lifetime when you do. Before rushing in, perhaps we can learn to slow down and to truly listen to what people have to say to get to know an individual better. Who knows, we might even find a friend or lover in new, unexpected places!

Romantic Relationships

When it comes to Lagom and romantic relationships, there are a few key aspects to consider when trying to strengthen a bond with a loved one. Whether it be by being honest, listening to what they have to say, or giving them your undivided attention. These are just a few mentionable ways in which we can strengthen our relationships and form deeper bonds.

Listening

If you have perhaps conversed with a Swede, you'll notice that they rarely interrupt or talk over anyone else. Voices are kept at even tones, and pauses in conversations are entirely acceptable.

To the Brits, this can sometimes be seen as excruciatingly awkward. In today's day and age, we are so concerned about a gap in the conversation that we tend to constantly overlap people before they have had time to complete their sentences.

Swedes feel slightly awkward in these silent moments too, but instead of desperately trying to fill in the gap, the Swedes will opt to make a sound. (hmmm) This gives them time to reflect on the sentence (if needed) and reply with an adequate response.

Honesty

Most Swedes call it honesty; however, my English friends call it being 'direct'- either way, you'll only ever hear the truth from a Swede more often than most. Rather an honest "no" than an insincere "yes."

Take, for instance; a Swede notices your new haircut; they'd never go as far as to say that your haircut looks great when it clearly doesn't (unless they know you extremely well.) Although this would be the polite way to do things, they'll keep silent. This Lagom way of being honest (not too over honest) means you can fully trust a Swede.

This may seem hurtful at first, but at least you won't be walking around with a disastrous haircut for the next few months. Remember this for the next time you ask your friend for their honest opinion.

Being Punctual

I'm pretty ashamed to admit that there's one thing I've been known for, and that's my poor timekeeping skills. Having acknowledged this doesn't make it acceptable; however, I know I'm not alone in this.

Whether it be by going to the gym, school, work, or perhaps a party, people worldwide are showing up later and later than before. There is, however, an exception; Sweden.

Organize a dinner party, and you'll have guests showing up before you've finished tying your hair. In a nation where respect is high on the agenda and punctuality is critical, there are many positive incentives to be more punctual and to show that we care. However, social norms vary from country to country.

Six Reasons to Turn up on Time:

1. You'll keep the Swedes happy
2. You'll set an exemplary example for your kids and others around you
3. It'll make you feel more organized and calmer
4. It makes you appear more professional and dignified
5. It shows your trustworthy
6. It demonstrates kindness and respect for others

Undivided Attention

How distracting is a mobile phone? If you'd have to ask me that question, I'd say it's pretty distracting indeed. However, today's social psychologists are advising people on leaving their phones at home or at the very least at the bottom of their bag, but why is this?

To put it simply, our phones are a big distraction in our everyday lives, from constant social media notifications to checking our emails. Due to this, we might offend someone who's talking to you whilst talking on your phone (could be a friend, family, loved one, or perhaps even a stranger.)

I've noticed that even though occasionally you'll find a Swede with their phone on the table, it's generally turned on silent or face down to show a sign of respect. We can all take from this and become more present in the conversation, as well as show them that you have their undivided attention.

So rather than whipping out the phone as your friend goes to grab a coffee, sit back, relax and reflect on the conversation or perhaps take in the atmosphere.

Parenting

What if I told you that you don't need to be an all dancing, all singing super parent to be a good parent. In fact, our children will benefit significantly from moderation. By placing less stress and pressure on our little ones, we give them more space and time to blossom. I firmly believe that this will help you and your child find a greater balance.

One-on-one Time

As parents, we usually run around frantically, attempting to balance home, work, errands, and everything in between. Due to this, taking time out of the day is not always on the agenda. However, spending time with our kids doesn't necessarily have to be jam-packed with activities.

Simply setting aside a few moments of your day to spend time with them will greatly impact their self-esteem. In the spirit of Lagom, providing your kid/kids with simple but special one-on-one time is likely one of the very best gifts you can possibly give them.

Just by saying your door is always open to them or if you need someone to talk to, I'm here for you is a great way to start. This expectation eases the pressure on you as a parent (and the parental guilt we feel so very often), but it will also give your child the attention they crave and desire.

This time of day will more than likely become the most treasured time of day that you both share.

Parental Leave

Wander around any Swedish city at any given time of the day, and you'll notice men joyfully pushing prams, usually homemade and feeding their babies. The so-called 'Latte pappa' is a normal part of everyday life here in Sweden.

This is all thanks to Sweden's generous parental leave of 480 days, where both parents are encouraged to share it equally, and both parents can use it up until the child turns 12. It's been a common misconception around the world that women are more natural about parenting and enjoy it more than men do; however, this is certainly not the case.

I've spoken to many parents, both male and female, and most state that the amount of enjoyment is very much dependent on that individual. It's not about how much you enjoy it; it's simply about playing your part as a parent.

('Latte pappa' is the slang term for a very attractive and attentive Swedish dad.)

It's Good for Children to be Bored

It's relatively simple to get swept up in the idea that our children constantly need stimulation; however, I've noticed that the Swedes rarely overdo extracurricular activities. Experts have confirmed that 'quiet' time is equal if not more so crucial than organized activities.

This is because it gives your child time and space to develop essential life skills such as understanding emotions, forming friendships, and encouraging them to tap into their imagination.

So the very next time you hear your child complain about them being **"BOOORED!'** allow them to be just that. Chances are they'll think up their most creative and fun game yet!

Like the old Swedish proverb goes, "Those who wish to sing always find a song."

The Lagom Approach to Toys

We all, as parents, strive to ensure our child's needs are met and that they are happy. Not only by providing food, love, a home, and clothes but also with an occasional gift here and there to reward them for good behavior or an excellent report card at school.

Today, our children's bedrooms are stacked with toys that beep, sing and whistle but does that really make the little munchkins happier? Recently, I was quite shocked to discover that, according to experts, more toys or ones that aren't age-appropriate can do more harm than good.

So which toys should we invest in? As with all things Lagom, it's about finding balance and ensuring that the toy/toys should be age-appropriate.

(Usually, there is a label or sticker that indicates age, i.e., 6+)

How do I Choose The Right Toy?

When it comes to selecting the right toys for our children, it's tempting to go straight for the bright plastic ones. They almost whisper to you as you walk past, screaming, 'BUY ME!' but is this really the best option for your kid/kids?

In my opinion, "NO," the classic toys are generally the ones you'll get the most mileage on. These can be anything from teddy bears, lego, *train sets, wooden building blocks, and other constructive toys.*

Note: You must always watch your child while they play with lego or any small toy, as these small items if swallowed or ingested, can cause fatal injuries.

These toys will encourage creativity and can help improve problem-solving skills. Why not consider investing in some homemade, beautifully hand-crafted items instead of plastic ones, as your child/children can enjoy these toys over the many years to come.

Five Things to Look for In a Child's Toy:

1. The toy doesn't over entertain (i.e., Flash, beep, or play music)
2. Your child can use it as they get older
3. Helps stimulate imagination
4. It helps stimulate exploratory play
5. Has more than one use (can be used time and time again)

Dressing-up Box

I absolutely adore seeing my little ones all dolled up in their hand-picked items from the dress-up box.

In my mind, the best boxes have extravagant, flamboyant pieces like traditional costumes picked up on family travels and vacations. These items can be anything from your old jacket and jewelry to wacky hats, and sunglasses picked up from second-hand stores.

Don't be shy, be bold. You'll end up taking some pictures and having memories that'll last a lifetime.

(Let's not forget to mention that you'll have a couple of embarrassing pictures that you can show to their friends or loved ones, just putting it out there)

Children and The Great Outdoors

Let's face it: few children greet the "let's go outside to play" with shouts of joy.

They won't necessarily admit this, but your kid/kids certainly do love this interaction you are giving them. Even small activities such as playing in the garden or walking in the park can greatly impact your child's self-esteem.

Those are just two simple activities that you can do with your kid/kids; as I know, setting an entire day aside might seem like an impossible feat to most.

10 Creative Activities for You and Your Child to Do Outdoors

1. Have fun finding and identifying different trees
2. Sow some seeds and get your kids interested in gardening (as I'm sure they'd love to get their hands dirty)
3. Build a sand or mud castle
4. Get your hands dirty and make some mud pies
5. Teach your children about the outdoors and some survival skills (i.e., making a fire or learning how to fish)
6. Make a daisy chain or a dandelion crown.
7. Point out the names of different plants and wildlife
8. Collect leaves and other small items to create a collage at home.

9. Go shell-seeking (at the beach)
10. Run through the alphabet, asking your child or children to collect small pieces from the wild, starting with the letter 'A' and so on.

Top Tip: *If you are really serious about getting your child to interact with the great outdoors more, you can always look at putting your child/children in a Forest school. It would be in your best interest to enquire with your local school if they perhaps have such activities or classes, as some schools may not have the facilities or offer those classes.*

Make sure to run it by your child/children to see if they'd like to go to such a school as their future dreams or aspirations might be affected by you choosing what you want your child to pursue, instead of letting them have free rain over their career choice in the near future.

Dress for The Occasions

In Sweden, spending time with your children isn't confined to fair-weather days; this can be said for other countries too. Except there's a significant difference when it comes to dressing children for the weather, as the Swedes can firmly hold this down.

I marvel at how the Swedes dress their kids for the weather. Every season brings a new collection of appropriate attire, be it a pair of boots, a full-body snowsuit, or a spring hat.

The Lagom Guide to Dressing your child for The Cold Winter:

- Ideal temperature: 68°F or 20°C
- Cool top with long sleeves or a shirt that covers the shoulders
- Feet covers such as wetsuit shoes (if on the beach) or surf shoes
- Rash vest if you are perhaps on the beach
- Sunglasses
- Sunscreen
- Neck cover or sun hat (sun hats can come with additional neck covers)
- Ideal temperature: 40-60°F or 5-15°C (Everyday)
- Thin hat
- Thin gloves

- Tough waterproof trousers
- Ideal temperature: 40-60°F or 5-15°C (If Raining)
- Wellington boots
- Waterproof Anorak with hood
- Waterproof trousers
- Ideal temperature: 32°F or 0°C (If Snowing)
- Waterproof snow boots
- Neck Warmer or scarf
- Snowsuit
- Ski socks
- Base layer
- Mid Layer
- Outer layer

Learning The Lagom Way

It's amazing how many parents start teaching their children to read and write before their school life even starts. One of the many things I've come to love about Swedish parenting is this: I rarely experience any parents boasting about their child being able to read or write from an early age. Neither is there any parental competitiveness if you know what I mean.

Six Important Things to Teach Your Children Before School:

1. How to be thankful
2. How to share
3. How to be a good fiends
4. How to be kind and caring
5. How to have respect
6. How to stand up for themselves and or others

Letting Your Child Take the Lead

Swedish children start compulsory school from the age of seven, two years later than their UK counterparts. Up until then, the focus is purely focused on stimulation and play.

In fact, a study has shown that children that learn to read and write at a later stage are no less successful than peers who start earlier. I've learned as a parent that trying to teach them too early can cause a considerable amount of stress and aggravation for both you and the little one.

So slow down and take things at your child's pace; you'll be surprised at the positive effects this can have on your child.

(As the old Swedish proverb goes; "Even the smallest of stars shines in the darkness.')

Ease The Pressure

This Slower way of learning should continue all the way up until primary school. The focus is to learn without the pressure of achieving top grades. Additionally, the focus is also on helping children discover the pleasure of learning by working in groups or pairs rather than insisting that they compete against each other.

I understand all too well that we can't control the age at which our children start compulsory school nor the teaching philosophy. However, taking the Lagom approach is a great way to guide and encourage our children, but first and foremost, to show them unconditional love.

Be a parent that's non-judgemental and accept and try to understand that they'll have strengths and weaknesses.

Pink and Blue

Sweden is known for being the most gender-equal country; they believe that gender equality starts from the day you are born. The idea is to introduce the baby to the world without having a set gender-specific toy/toys.

By doing so, you encourage them to enjoy the world around them based on their natural preferences. In the same vein, a lot can be said about providing your children with opportunities, regardless of their sex.

So, the next time you're buying toys for your little one, try not categorizing them like toys for 'boys' and toys for 'girls.' Let's start allowing children to be children regardless of whatever choice they might make.

Friendships

When it comes to Lagom and friendships, the concept of not too much, not too little can apply tremendously.

How do you ask? To put it simply, by having a Lagom way of thinking, you can strengthen bonds and relationships and get to know certain individuals better. What's more Lagom than that?

How To Entertain The Lagom Way

Due to the high taxes in Sweden, drinking and eating out has always been a costly affair. Although it is more affordable these days, most Swedes opt to meet up at the house instead of in town. Home entertainment is usually a relatively informal affair. The primary factor here is to keep it simple.

I've been to countless dinner parties hosted by some of my most dear Swedish friends, and I can tell you that the meal was terrific. However, it is not uncommon to suggest a get-together where everyone chips in with whatever they might have in the fridge. The result is a fuss-free, relaxed and calm event, where everyone has a Lagom amount to do. So why not host a get-together with some friends and family? It'll be great for everyone!

The next time you put off a get-together with friends and family due to time, budget, or energy, how about trying one of the four following ideas:

Build a bonfire:

In Spring, Swedes who live in apartments with communal gardens set aside a date to prepare the garden for the outdoor season. Whether you have your own garden or perhaps share a flat or apartment, why not grab some friends and have some fun cleaning up around the garden.

You can rake up some leaves, clear the moss out or the gutters or simply sweep the driveway. After you've finished cleaning, you can chuck all the old sticks and dry grass/leaves on top of the bonfire. Just make sure it's a small load at a time to reduce the risk of the fire spreading.

Waffle afternoon:

Forget about the high tea in Sweden; if it's not a Fika, then it's all about the waffles. The beauty of them is that they're incredibly simple to make; simply pour readymade or homemade batter over a waffle iron. Easy to serve and popular among all ages as well. Try spice things up and add some Lingonberry jam to the top or perhaps some maple syrup.

Barbeque:

Clean out your grill for a relaxed get-together. You can do this in the safety of your back garden, the woods, or at the beach. It's not about wowing people with butter-fried shrimp cocktails or popping a champagne bottle. Rather it's about keeping it hassle-free, with everyone providing something to throw on the grill. You don't have to be shy either to invite a colleague or a next-door neighbor, small acts of generosity will always go a long way.

This doesn't have to stop there either; try hosting your own barbeque get-together with friends and family, maybe try asking your crush if she'd like to attend. Who knows, she might even say yes!

Picnics:

Picnics are an ideal easy meal that you can share with plenty in the warmer months. They require little in the way of planning and preparation and can be enjoyed practically everywhere. This activity can be a great source of fun for you and the little munchkins. Just keep your fingers crossed that the rain will hold up, and it will be a wonderful, beautiful day spent outside.

Celebrations

Never is the Lagom philosophy more evident than when it comes to celebrations. Christmas, midsummer, and Easter tend to be relaxed affairs.

Lagom is geared towards being together by keeping the cost down and sharing the load. Gifts are picked to be just right for the occasion and wrapped in simple, understated paper. Decoration is an equally delicate balance, so don't overdo it, and it might seem vulgar to underdo it, and it won't look *festligt* (party-like).

Christmas

Although we all have our own family traditions, perhaps I'm not quite ready to pull out a turkey with some pickled herrings. However, I quite admire the way my family-in-laws organize and plan. Each individual must bring at least one item to the table, quite literally.

I've noticed that helping to contribute by bringing food, drinks, or snacks is commonplace for the Swedes. Dividing up tasks not only eases some of the pressure off the host, but it also means everyone has a sense of responsibility.

Sharing out responsibilities such as preparing the dishes, serving the drinks, choosing the music, or perhaps organizing a treasure hunt ensures that everyone has just the Lagom amount to do. By doing so, no one is out of pocket, and it becomes a more relaxed and laid-back affair.

Understated decorations

When it comes to decorations and Christmas in Sweden, there's a distinct serenity and coziness, with also a strong sense of nostalgia.

On the whole, Father Christmas climbing up the chimney and colored flashing lights are strictly out of bounds. I don't even want to begin to think about what would happen if you put a 10-foot or three-meter inflatable snowman in your garden.

Instead, think more along the lines of fairy lights that give off a soft glow, flickering candles, vintage decorations, tablecloths that have been passed down from generation to generation, and handmade and natural touches from right outside your front door.

The Rustic Christmas Tree

There's generally a Christmas-tree frenzy in the days running up to Christmas, with everyone in search of the perfect pine (not too tall, not too wide, just right!). But what if I told you that the more imperfect the tree, the better. Yes, you read that correctly. Since many Swedes chop down their own trees, it can be a case of using whatever has grown in the garden over the years.

Even if the tree is purchased locally or at a farm, there is still a big emphasis on imperfection. In fact, some individuals shun the conical-shaped pine and opt for a *Lebanese cedar tree* (very popular in Denmark). The tree itself is reasonably crooked and far from perfect; however, this tree is incredibly charming and has plenty of benefits.

The spacing between the branches means you'll have no problem placing decorations that will be seen more clearly, and it also allows space for real candles. (*Ensure that the candle/candles are placed safely to prevent a fire from breaking out!*) By picking up an imperfect tree, you'll add a bucket-load of rusticity and charm to your home at Christmas.

If you'd like to add an extra Swedish touch, you can always search 'Scandinavian Christmas Tree' and look for other ideas to really spruce things up! One of the best tricks I've learned while choosing a Christmas tree is that you should look for a tree planted in a pot rather than being cut off from the stem. Moreover, finding a tree with roots is ideal as you can replant it the following year.

Chopping Down Your Christmas Tree

With an abundant forest right in front of most Swedes' homes, it's not uncommon for them to saw down a tree in their garden or visit a local Christmas-tree store.

Sustainable Christmas-tree farms are becoming more and more popular across Europe and beyond. So why not go out and chop a tree down yourself, or perhaps you're like me and prefer to take the Lagom approach to things (store-bought tree)? Either way, both are Lagom.

Crafting

Swedes love to *pysslar* (get creative) before any major holiday. They generally set aside a day to make decorations and bake as a family during the month. To *julpysslar* (create Christmas crafts) may involve making a candle wreath, paper stars, or perhaps even a gingerbread house.

The beauty in this is that the creations don't necessarily have to be perfect, just Lagom. In fact, the more rustic, the better. It's simply about getting together and enjoying the moment.

Natural Hand-made Decorations

Many of my Swedish friends love to forage local and seasonal items like holly springs, pine cones, acorn cups (which they'll use as centerpieces), and this will add a decorative touch to your home/apartment.

Usually, Christmas decorations start going up by the first day of *Advent*. Although subtle, homemade seasonal wreaths that are hanging on the door will add a warm welcome long before this.

Natural hand-made items are all about keeping the look simple and letting the shape of the freshly cut foliage speak for itself.

A Christmas Wreath Inspired by Nature

To create that immediate sense of holiday spirit, hang a homemade wreath on your window or on the door. This task does not have to be difficult. In fact, the simpler it is, the more charming and welcoming it will feel!

The Hanging-candle Wreath:

A simple flickering candle on the window can brighten up even the bleakest of days. This simple candle wreath is relatively easy to make and looks stunning while hanging on the window. Once finished, light the candle and watch the magic start!

What You Need:

- Small candle
- Clip-on candle holder
- Leather or twine for hanging
- Round metal frame or coat a coat hanger bent into the shape of the desired candle.
- Wire cutters
- Green garden wire

A bundle of *Eucalyptus* foliage about six sprigs or more depending on candle size (you can also use spruce, boxwood, or anything else that's in season and readily available)

What To Do:

Take your three sprigs of foliage and carefully bind them with your garden wire at the stem.

Use a piece of wire to fix the bundle to the metal frame.

Create a new foliage bundle using the remaining three sprigs of foliage and make a bundle that overlaps the tips of the first bundle to hide the wire, then fasten in place with more wire.

Continue until you've covered at least half of the circle.

Measure the height in which you'll be hanging the wreath, and then attach the leather, string, or wire to the top half of the metal frame.

Add the clip-on candle holder to the center of the bottom half of the wreath. Then fix the candle into the candle-holder, hang the wreath vertically on your window or door and watch it twinkle.

CHAPTER 4: PRACTICE AND LIVE LAGOM

When it comes to Lagom as a whole, there are plenty of things that you can do the Lagom way to help better our environment and, in turn, live a happier lifestyle.

Respecting nature, establishing communities, saving energy at work and home, and reducing our carbon footprint are all ways in which we can live an eco-daily life. These are but just a few of the many other ways to practice and live lagom.

The Environment and Sustainability

When looking at the environment and sustainability, we, as inelegant beings, know all too well about the earth's repercussions if we do not choose to live in a sustainable and environmentally friendly way.

From climate change up to global warming, the effects that have been seen in the past couple of years show us just how important it is to start living a more eco-friendly lifestyle.

You can do this through small and subtle changes like turning off the lights or closing the tap to save water. These small tasks can and will make a difference, not to mention reduce your carbon footprint at the same time. So don't leave that geyser on; instead, switch it off!

Respecting Nature

You can accomplish this in a multitude of ways when it comes to respecting nature. Why should we respect nature?

You may be wondering, well, that is quite a simple question. At any given moment in time, the earth's surface is being disrupted at an alarmingly rapid pace.

From deforestation to cultivation and urbanisation, the effects and consequences will become tremendous if we do not implement eco-friendly ways. This will be devastating. It's sad to think about the effect that can be had on certain living species and, in some more severe cases, extinction!

Attracting The Birds and The Bees

Not an insect person? Well, neither am I; however, I will say that ever since I've added a couple of seasonal flowers and roses into my garden, it's been buzzing, quite literally.

Why, you may ask? Well, simply put, we need those tiny creatures, some are pollinators, and others are food sources in some countries. These little critters play a crucial role in maintaining the ecosystem and keeping everything in check. So if you were perhaps wondering, yes, we do play an essential role in all of this, and it's up to us and the future generations to help preserve what little species and wildlife we have left.

Seriousness aside, for now, there are, however, things that you can do in the comfort of your own home/apartment that can help leave a positive carbon footprint on the earth's surface.

By doing your part, you help create a slice of heaven for all little insects, no matter how big or small.

Go Wild

At our family summer cottage, my father-in-law would always leave a section of lawn completely untouched. This would come across as a surprise to most as this indeed was to me, as I was used to the pristinely cut laws that I'd come across at most European homes/households.

Until I discovered that there's a very sound principle to this madness, untouched areas leave space for tiny insects and critters to go about their work undisturbed. Long grass, for example, is akin to a mini jungle or forest that helps nurture flowers, pollen, and seeds.

In turn, this attracts insects, moths, and many other various types of species, such as birds and monkeys (if found in your area) or perhaps even the local town hedgehog named; Frank.

Two Simple Ideas:

1. *Go native and be diverse:* You'll attract more native wildlife this way. You can even plant a diverse range of shrubs and trees. It would be in your best interest to stick to native plant species. This will ensure that no specific plant becomes dominant and everything thrives.

2. *Add a water feature:* A simple hand-built pond, birdbath, or container of water placed outside will attract a couple of creatures, from toads to frogs, as well as birds and other passing wildlife that might be thirsty for a drink.

Feed The Birds!

Give birds a helping hand and get in touch with nature a little by leaving out some bird food/seeds.

Opt for a variety of feeders to increase your chances of spotting various species of birds. (*keep an eye out for local squirrels as they might want to get into these feeders. If so, you can always invest in a bird feeder that spins. From what I can tell you, it's hours and hours of laughter worth every penny!*)

You might even consider taking up bird watching as a pastime or hobby, and there is nothing wrong with that!

The Insect Hotel

With urban areas constantly expanding, many insects and local wildlife are losing their homes. This poses a severe threat to our ecosystem, as many insects and creatures help keep the world in balance.

You'll be surprised to know that the Swedish city of *Mölndal* has taken significant measures to combat this insect housing problem. As much as you love animals, if you live in a small home/apartment, you tend to value the little space you have. Due to this, we tend to forget the little creatures and insects that called this their 'home' before us.

Just a little something to ponder when you walk into your newly built home. So, create an insect hotel or get a carpenter to design and build one, as I'm sure the creepy-crawlers will love it.

Help Save The Bees!

There's been a rapid decline in the number of bees since the nineties due to parasites, climate change, and industrial agriculture.

According to the Swedish beekeeping association, we should be concerned about our black and yellow friends. *Reportedly 76% of everything grown in Europe can be attributed to the pollination and hard work of the bees.*

Four Simple Ways to Help Save The Bees:

1. You can create a bee-friendly garden by planting specific plants like herbs, vegetables, and fruit.
2. Buy organic honey
3. Stick to honey labeled 'non-transformed' and 'non-heated.'
4. Buy fresh honey and support the local farms and beekeepers in your area

Bee Loving Flowers and Plants to Plant in Your Garden

Fruits & Vegetables:

- Cucumber
- Blackberries
- Pumpkins
- Strawberries
- Wild garlic
- Annuals:
- Cleome
- Clover
- Poppy
- Sunflower
- Borage
- Perennials:
- Dahlia
- Rose
- Snowdrop
- Foxglove
- Crocus
- Buttercup
- Geranium
- Herbs:
- Coriander
- Fennel
- Lavender
- Sage
- Mint
- Thyme
- Catnip

Protect The Trees!

It's not uncommon to encounter a local Swede who owns a piece of wooded land in the forests of Sweden. More than 50% of the county is covered in a thick blanket of forest.

The scenery is beautiful, so we need to try our hardest to preserve it. You can help in many ways, such as keeping your community tidy, recycling, reducing your packaging waste, and reusing old rubbish. It's never too late to begin, so you best get moving!

Keep Your Community Tidy!

As I'm sure you are well aware by now, the Swedes are incredibly tidy people. Their fever for orderliness extends to the public domain, too.

Put simply, Sweden is rather immaculate. They even have government clean-up services; however, this does not diminish people's effort by doing their bit. The Swedes take pride in keeping their public spaces clean, whether that be by keeping the local toilets or city parks clean.

By tidying up after yourself, you ensure that your wastage can harm no animal or insect, so be a 'Karen' if needed and tell your little ones that their rubbish should be thrown away and discarded correctly. Doing this sets an excellent example for your children and impacts the future generation positively.

If you'd like to help out even more and become a little more productive, you can always participate in community clean-up events.

Recycling

Recycling is nothing new; however, it's just as important as any other of the previously mentioned topics and topics to come. By sorting and recycling through our rubbish, we ensure that as many of our recyclable materials are being reused and recycled correctly.

Ultimately reducing the need to extract new raw materials and limiting the amount of waste that ends up in our beautiful blue oceans!

Reducing Your Packaging Waste!

Nothing can shout 'I'm eco-friendly!' more than a reusable shopping bag when it comes to packaging waste.

Not only does using a reusable plastic bag cut down on plastic waste, but it also reduces CO2 emissions that are made during the manufacturing process. On the other hand, packaging has been a huge problem and will be for many years to come.

However, many different companies and brands have hopped on the eco-friendly bandwagon, dramatically decreasing our overall wastage.

Five Simple Ways To Reduce Your Packaging Waste:

1. Make your favorite brew of tea using loose tea leaves instead of teabags
2. Take a travel mug with you to coffee shops to avoid disposable cups
3. Use your own water bottle instead of buying a new one (which most of us are guilty of)
4. Go for bulk buys instead of individually wrapped items
5. Opt for items that are refundable and reusable

Reuse Your Rubbish!

I know what most of us would be thinking, "Ewww gross!" and I wouldn't fault you for thinking like this, as reusing your old rubbish would pretty much make any individual sick to their stomach.

However, why not tap into your inner creative self and give your rubbish a new lease on life? You can even ask a local school if they need any craft supplies.

(As many of these items that we throw away, i.e., plastic bottles, containers, old clothes, and cardboard boxes, can be utilized for a school art project or donated to "eco-drives.")

Establishing Yourself in A Community

There's deliberate unselfishness about Lagom that has been around for centuries, even since the Viking times.

Back then, it was as straightforward as passing around a cup of mead and ensuring everyone had Lagom. Today, it can be linked to working towards a fairer society. This ensures that no one goes without. This can be done whether you donate money, volunteer, or genuinely make an effort to be kind to those around you.

By working collectively, we can foster a happier, healthier community.

Thinking of Others

You can say a fair amount about an individual who cares about others, especially in today's day and age where everyone's wandering around in their own little bubbles, drowning in a sea of emails.

We are quite often caught up in our own troubles that we simply can't find the time nor have the patience to deal with others. According to an old Swedish proverb, *'one must learn to make others happy if one wants to be happy.'*

As a study by Harvard *Business School* claims, this just goes to show that helping other people does indeed make you happier.

Helping Those in Need

I generally find the Swedes to be a little shy, especially in public places. You'll rarely see a smile from a stranger, especially in the bigger cities in Sweden.

The same can be said about speaking. Very few words are exchanged on the streets. But don't be mistaken; behind that cool veneer lies a heart of gold. Take, for instance, Sweden's reputation for being one of Europe's most welcoming countries for refugees. This open mindset is reinforced with compassion and a willingness to help.

So take the time out of your day and donate to a local 'volunteers club.' Perhaps even help them out if they require a pair of helping hands. Small acts of generosity can go quite the distance!

Become A Volunteer

We all know that volunteer work is a great way to give back to the community; however, this is often a nagging thought in our minds.

Just another item on the list of the many other things to do. A common misconception is that we need loads of free time to spare, to participate in these kinds of activities. You can do plenty of volunteering activities during specific time frames.

You can also inquire what times you'll be looking at, so plan ahead and start sowing that seed!

Five Great Ways to Help in Your Community:

1. Contact your local authority, inquire about local volunteer opportunities in your area, and perhaps see if something piques your interests.
2. Find a local charity that you're interested in and ask them if you can help or be of any assistance. If you can donate, well, there is that option too!
3. Help out at a children's sports club, whether that be by serving drinks to the little ones or frying up hotdogs on the BBQ to raise money.
4. Visit a local liberty and sign up for a support group. You could possibly teach English or your mother tongue to new people entering the country.
5. Visit a nursing home and ask if they perhaps need any assistance; this can be as simple as sweeping rooms out to mopping floors. If you know you can handle more, you can always enquire and ask for a change in job duties, but at the end of the day, it's the thought that counts.

Random Acts of Kindness

As with all things Lagom, spreading happiness, grand gestures, and over-the-top planning are all part of the mindset.

A simple random act of kindness can show strong character in yourself and/or other individuals. Sometimes the most ordinary of simple acts of kindness add the most meaning and can inspire the most incredible smiles of all.

These simple, thoughtful acts can end up brightening someone else's day. I'm sure that you're already a kind and caring individual; however, a gentle reminder to be aware of others surely doesn't go unnoticed.

Five Random Acts of Kindness:

1. Carry a spare umbrella and lend it to a friend when it rains
2. Write a handwritten letter to a friend, relative, or loved one
3. Write a thank-you note to the public services such as the police, nurses, and firefighters
4. Try giving out ten heartfelt compliments a day
5. Leave a sweet note inside a library book for the next reader

Saving Energy at Home The Lagom Way!

You need only turn on your t.v. to see just how severe the effects of climate change are having on the environment and the many other different species.

It's easy to think along the lines that recycling, reusing, and reducing our waste are all futile efforts in the way of stopping climate change. However, this is not the case as we can implement other effective ways into our daily lives to make a difference. This will reduce our carbon footprint and ultimately save energy the Lagom way.

So just imagine what we could all achieve if we just tackle what we can the Lagom way and take small, simple steps.

Start Small

It's really quite incredible how many things can be done at home to save energy and reduce CO2 emissions.

From keeping your house warm and cool, the Swedish way to saving water, and so much more are all effective ways in which we can start small. It's as simple as turning off your tap while you brush your teeth (A rule that was regularly enforced in my household). While starting small can be done in numerous ways, it's still up to you to make the change.

Like the old Swedish proverb says, *"A journey of a thousand miles always begins with a single step."*

Get To the Source

In Sweden, the hydro, wind, and solar power energy account for 52% of the electricity used in Sweden.

This gives the Swedes the right to brag about their county being number one in the world for sustainable energy use. They're even on their way to becoming the first fossil-free nation. This just goes to show how eco-friendly the Swedes actually are. Luckily in these times, we are fortunate enough to choose the energy providers that we will be partnering with.

So do some background research and find out whether the energy providers that you are going to go with are eco-friendly or, at the very least, the company is trying to go green/greener.

You can always choose to go with a company that uses more renewable resources.

Keep Your House Warm and Cool the Swedish Way

When my mother-in-law comes to spend the night, she always brings her thermal pajamas only to complain about it being too hot the following morning.

The Swedes go to great lengths to ensure that their homes are at just the right temperature, not too hot, not too cold. A well-insulated house can have numerous advantages in a hot or cold climate.

Let's not forget to mention that this can keep you nice and cozy during the winter or cool and refreshed during the summer.

Your Home-energy Use

Heating accounts for a shocking 42% of the energy used in the average U.K. home. The environmental impact and quickly escalating costs.

This is even more of a reason to start following the example of the Swedish by checking if we retain heat in the most efficient of ways. Sometimes investments are required; however, these pay off in the long run.

Even the smallest of steps can assist you in turning your home into an energy-efficient household, which will, in turn, save you a few pennies too!

Layer Up!

Suppose you are not too sure about making a significant insulation investment or are lucky enough to stay in a climate where extreme measures aren't necessary

. In that case, you can just add some curtains, blinds, a simple furry rug, or perhaps a couple of candles to add that warm sense of feeling to your home/apartment. These simple items help amp up that cozy feeling that you might want to achieve if you, perhaps, stay in a cooler climate.

After all, the philosophy of Lagom isn't about making things perfect; it's about putting in just the right amount of effort to ensure that you and or your loved ones are comfortable.

Wrap Up!

According to a report from the *U.K. government's Department of Energy and Climate Change*, dialing down the thermometer by just 68°F or 28°C to 64°F or 18°C degrees is the number one thing you can do to reduce and save energy at home.

The report also recommended that you delay turning on your heater by a month (from October to November) and turning off unused radiators in empty rooms.

So go and grab that sweater or jump into a warm set of clothes; winters coming!

Three Ways to Keep the Heat Indoors:

1. If your home has a fireplace, ensure that the damper is working
2. Eliminate draughts from doors and windows
3. Ensure that your walls, ceiling, floors, and loft are well insulated

Shutting The Doors on Goodbyes

Whenever guests leave our house in the winter, my mother-in-law quickly dashes over to close the door right behind them.

This seemed quite rude for me as I was not yet accustomed to the way the Swedes do things here, even after a couple of years of staying there.

However, to be quite frank, there's a message to be heard behind this madness. Simply put, the warm air inside the house doesn't escape, and that chilly winter breeze doesn't blow in.

So next time you invite guests over for the winter, save the goodbyes for inside.

Adopt New Energy-Saving Habits

It's easy to forget at times that everything we do, from going about our daily lives to ordering a coffee, uses energy.

These actions play a small part (but a role all the same) in using up the world's finite natural resources. Now I won't suggest to you that you need to start feeling your way around the house with the lights off.

However, you can keep them off and reduce energy usage by placing some candles in a few strategic spots around your home/apartment. This will ultimately cut down on energy usage and help you save some money too.

Go Natural!

To reduce the overall amount of energy you use, how about you start shining a light on the Swedish way of doing things.

Start by making the maximum use of light by placing items that require plenty of light (i.e., the sofa or dining table for reading/eating) by windows to cut down on artificial light. By doing so, not only will your effort be gentler on your pocket, but this will also help reduce the impact you have on the planet.

So, start going natural and make full use of that empty space in front of the window. It hasn't been sitting there empty for nothing!

Make The Change!

Lighting is something of a necessity. It aids us in seeing what we are doing and creates a wonderfully warm and cozy atmosphere at home.

This comes as no real shock to me as seeing that the average household contains, on average, "42" lights, and if we are speaking about cost, well, then that's going to be quite costly, to say the least.

According to a report done by *Energimyndigheten* (*The Swedish Energy Agency*), light bulbs account for one-fifth of the global electricity used. Most of which comes from nonrenewable resources.

Experts suggest that by changing from traditional incandescent light bulbs to more efficient energy-saving light bulbs such as; CFL, LED, or halogen incandescents; you'll use up to 25-80% less energy.

These light bulbs will also last you up to 25 times longer than your traditional light bulb.

Five Small Energy Saving Habits That One Can Adopt:

1. ***Skip The Dryer:*** Save energy by drying your clothes on the clothesline, in the garden, or on a drying rack, rather than using a tumble dryer. This will also help to cut down on energy consumption and help your clothes last longer too!

2. ***Stain-spot Clothes:*** Back in the old days, plenty of clothes were hand-washed, which enabled them to get more wear out of the clothes. So why not think along the same lines and hand-wash some items. This will save time, energy, and money, but this way of cleaning is way less detrimental to the planet. You

could even give them a good steam by hanging them by the shower, just putting it out there.

3. ***Boil What You Need:*** The *U.K. Tea and Infusion Association* calculated that the Brits, on average, gulp down 165 million cups of tea every day. Three out of four individuals admit they overfill their kettles each time. It's been estimated that the combined average British household could possibly save 68 million pounds on energy a year.

4. ***Unplug At The source:*** According to the *U.S. Department of Energy*, 75% of our electrical appliances consume energy while we are not at home. This can be a serious problem when it draws closer to the end of the month when rent is due. The electricity used from our appliances while we are away at work or on vacations can drastically increase your overall energy usage. This means the energy bill will go up too. However, this is a relatively easy problem to fix simply unplug all electrical devices from the wall ensuring no energy is being wasted, solving the high electricity bill problem.

5. ***Flip The Switch:*** In our daily rush to get home in the morning after work, it's easy to forget about the lights and leave them on. (I've been guilty of this too, on many occasions) What difference do a few light bulbs make, right? A shocking 90% of the energy used by incandescent light bulbs is released through heat, and the higher the wattage, the more energy that is used. So turn those lights off, and you'll save in many more ways than one.

Save Water!

Whenever I'm brushing my teeth or washing my face, the tap is always turned off after using it.

This has become almost second nature for me, not only because it saves water but also cuts down on my monthly water bill. Many of us aren't fully aware of just how much water we use when we water the garden, flush the toilet or take our daily shower.

Reducing Your Foodprint The Lagom Way!

Food, what's not to love? I'm quite the foodie if I do say so myself, and at any given time of day, I love indulging in some of my favorite snacks.

It's essential to eat in moderation to limit the effect that our eating habits have on the planet. So why not follow the example set by the Swedes by enjoying a vegetarian meal, decluttering your kitchen, or perhaps taking the food leftover to work, ensuring that nothing goes to waste.

In this way, we can all reduce our footprint while still enjoying a *härlig måltid! (Tasty Meal)*

Preparing & Cooking Food the Energy-Efficient Way

The kitchen has always been known as the heart of the kitchen, and for a good reason.

This is where the magic happens and where drinks, food, and conversations are made. But did you know that this part of the kitchen is where we waste a huge portion of energy?

By making a few small changes in how we cook and prepare our food, you can save plenty of energy and precious time. By implementing a few energy-efficient ways into the kitchen, you'll feel more than welcome to indulge in that freshly baked cinnamon bun.

Five Ways to Become Energy-Efficient in The Kitchen:

1. ***Use A Dishwasher:*** If you fill a traditional dishwasher, it will use way less water and is more energy-efficient than the conventional method of tidying-up.

2. ***Keep The Oven Closed:*** It's pretty tempting to open the oven and check up on how that Sunday roast is coming along. But did you know that just by opening the oven door, you can lose up to 25% of the heat stored there? Try peeping through the glass next time, or perhaps set that timer that's been collecting dust for quite some time now.

3. ***Select The Correct Appliance:*** Opt for smaller appliances that keep energy consumption low. This will reduce the energy required for the meal you are preparing. There's always the other option of searching for items that come with energy-efficient labels.

4. ***Use The Right Pots and Pans:*** Invest in some quality cookware to improve heat conduction. Select the right size pan/pot for the meal that you're preparing, ensuring that you keep the lid on to retain the heat. You might even opt to invest in a pressure cooker, which has been said to cook meals up to 70% faster.

5. ***Keep It Simple:*** Look for recipes that require only one pot/pan. If you're thinking about cooking some pasta, you can always place the metal colander on top of the pot to steam the vegetables simultaneously.

Live Eco Daily The Lagom Way!

When we think of Lagom, the first thing that usually springs to mind is "Not too much, not too little."

This can be taken quite literally, from the way we save water up to living an eco-daily lifestyle, all factor in when trying to take the Lagom approach.

At the end of the day, it's not just about personal transport and manufacturing that contribute to the emissions of greenhouse gases. But the way in which we choose to live our lifestyles can also have drastic effects on the climate and ecosystem.

Eco-Friendly transport!

In Sweden, riding a bicycle is second nature.

It's simply a healthier and more practical way to travel, which helps cut down on CO_2 emissions that would have been produced (if you had taken the car or public transport). Sometimes, though, an ordinary bike isn't up to the task, whether because the distance is too far or simply the weather gods are just not on your side today.

If that is the scenario, then there are plenty of other options you can choose from, so let's look at a few.

The Freight-Bike:

Also known as the box or cargo bike, the freight bike is a compact and adapted bicycle with a front carrier designed to carry bigger loads without using a car.

From groceries to children, this nifty little bike is an efficient way in which you can transport goods across your local town—ultimately reducing your carbon footprint. Not to mention this gives your quads a good workout too. Who needs a gym anyway?

The Electric Bicycle:

Just the other day, I was racing alongside a bicycle path *malmö* (Late as usual) when I noticed an elderly gentleman casually pass me without breaking much of a sweat.

Me being as competitive an individual as I can be, I quickly peddled faster to regain my lost position. However, unfortunately, the old gentleman promptly peddled away into the distant sunset. (Slightly far-fetched, he kind of got away, so to say.) It was only later on in the day that I realized, thanks to a helpful friend pointing out, that the man was most probably on an e-bike.

Otherwise known as an eclectic bicycle. An e-bike is a fully customized bicycle that runs on electricity. More recent models have the option of having the battery recharged while you cycle to cut down on energy consumption.

This is a cleaner, greener, and less environmentally damaging way to travel.

Electric Cars:

Hybrid and electric cars are a hot topic in today's automotive industry.

With many companies trying to make their products greener, eco-friendly, and environmentally safe, the automotive industry decided that they, too, couldn't fall behind. With plenty of people raring towards becoming more eco-friendly, the craze over electric cars surely did not go unnoticed.

The fact that the electric car produces way less CO_2 emissions is just one of the many reasons to buy an electric vehicle.

Use Cars More Efficiently:

Even for the bike-crazed Swedes, using a bicycle is out of the option, and a car or local transportation service is needed.

Whether due to logistics, time, or the weather, there are always other ways to reduce the impact of CO_2 emissions. You can simply contact a work colleague and ask them if they can perhaps take you to work during the rainy season and if need be, you can always provide them with a transportations fee.

This cuts down on CO_2 emissions and dramatically reduces your carbon footprint. This is just one of the countless other options you can use when you want to cut down on those harmful emissions.

If you'd like to discover more effective ways on how to cut down on CO_2 emissions, you can always do some further research.

Public Transport:

When public transport springs to mind, the first thought is generally a huge bus, spewing out tons of harmful emissions.

However, these days, they're starting to clean up their act, with countless members of society becoming more and more aware of climate change and the effects that we are having on the environment.

This has prompted the public transportation sectors in most countries to start finding ways to cut down on greenhouse gases, ultimately providing better transportation services.

Eco-Friendly Shopping

According to the *IVL Swedish Environmental Research Institute*, every mobile phone produces a staggering 190lb (86kg) of emissions during the manufacturing process.

This is even before we take it out of the packaging, repair it or change it for a new one. One way in which we can become more eco-friendly is by buying less. This may seem hard to do. However, just remember that there are plenty of ways to acquire what you need without doing any unnecessary harm to the planet.

Buy Greener:

When it comes to buying greener, green stickers or eco-labels are the best way to go.

They are designed to make it easier for you, as the shopper, to consider the environment when making a buying/purchasing decision. By seeking out eco-friendly items, you subconsciously make a decision that's better for the planet and reduces the effects you have on the planet.

Since they're free of chemicals, they'll benefit your health too.

Buy Second Hand:

In Sweden, the vintage-clothing market has grown exponentially over the past few years, with many Swedes opting for second-hand goods over brand new ones.

By giving old clothes and items new life, you're saving the energy, and the time it would take to get here. Not to mention you'll be sporting an item that no one else has. Swedes love a bargain too, and will often hunt for bargains online or in local stores.

So don't feel shy to do the same!

Five Items Best Bought Used:

1. Sports Equipments And Musical Instruments
2. Jewelry
3. Children's clothes and toys
4. Bicycles
5. Art supplies such as canvas paper and old posters etc. (for the little ones' art projects)

Share and Share Alike

Sharing is a simple act of kindness and can be seen by many others as a sign that you've come from a good home.

This way of thinking has become second nature in my household, with my mother-in-law always asking the next-door neighbors if they perhaps need any kitchen or household supplies.

By doing so, you strengthen the bonds between yourself, neighbors, friends, and strangers. (who are more willing to trust you in their times of need) This is most probably why you can often see the Swedes passing goods and supplies over each other's fences with happy smiles adorning their faces.

CONCLUSION

Old Swedish proverb, *"The right amount is best."*

Writing this book has been quite the journey. Having lived in Sweden for quite some time now, I've slowly but steadily become more accustomed and accepting of Sweden's wonderful traditions.

Having conversed with quite a few of my Swedish friends before writing this book to get some insightful information. I realized that I am rather fortunate to be staying in this county that I now call home.

Even after having moved to Sweden, there are some old customs and practices that I simply can't shake off to this day, and you know what, that's perfectly "OK!." In other words, Lagom isn't about denying yourself life's simple pleasures; it's simply about enjoying everything in moderation just, Lagom!

Made in the USA
Coppell, TX
06 February 2023